Skills Builders

C000000919

YEAR 3

SPELLING AND VOCABULARY

Nicola Morris

Acknowledgements

Every effort has been made to trace all copyright holders, but if any have been inadvertently overlooked, the Publishers will be pleased to make the necessary arrangements at the first opportunity.

Although every effort has been made to ensure that website addresses are correct at time of going to press, Rising Stars cannot be held responsible for the content of any website mentioned in this book. It is sometimes possible to find a relocated web page by typing in the address of the home page for a website in the URL window of your browser.

Hachette UK's policy is to use papers that are natural, renewable and recyclable products and made from wood grown in well-managed forests and other controlled sources. The logging and manufacturing processes are expected to conform to the environmental regulations of the country of origin.

ISBN: 978-1-78339-709-9

Text, design and layout © 2019 Hodder & Stoughton Ltd.

First published in 2016 by Rising Stars, part of Hodder & Stoughton Ltd.
Rising Stars, An Hachette UK Company
Carmelite House 50 Victoria Embankment
London EC4Y 0DZ

www.risingstars-uk.com

All facts are correct at time of going to press.

Author: Nicola Morrris
Educational Consultant: Madeleine Barnes
Publisher: Laura White
Illustrator: Emily Skinner
Logo design: Amparo Barrera, Kneath Associates Ltd
Design: Julie Martin
Typesetting: Newgen
Cover design: Amparo Barrera, Kneath Associates Ltd
Project Manager: Seonaid Loader, Out of House Publishing
Copy Editor: Claire Pearce-Jones
Proofreader: Jennie Clifford
Software development: Alex Morris

All rights reserved. Apart from any use permitted under UK copyright law, no part of this publication may be reproduced

or transmitted in any form or by any means, electronic or mechanical, including photocopying and recording, or held within any information storage and retrieval system, without permission in writing from the publisher or under licence from the Copyright Licensing Agency Limited. Further details of such licences (for reprographic reproduction) may be obtained from the Copyright Licensing Agency Limited, https://www.cla.co.uk/

Pages that can be photocopied are clearly marked at the bottom of each page. The rights of Nicola Morris to be identified as the author of this work have been asserted by her in accordance with the Copyright, Design and Patents Act 1998.

British Library Cataloguing-in-Publication Data
A CIP record for this book is available from the British Library.
Printed in Dubai

Contents

All of the answers can be found online. To get access, simply register or login at **www.risingstars-uk.com**.

1 Vowels and consonants

The 26 letters of the alphabet are either **vowels** or **consonants**.
We often use these terms when talking about words and how
they are made up.

Vowels	a e i o u
Consonants	b c d f g h j k l m n p q r s t v w x y z

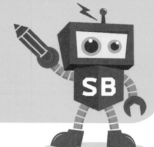

Activity 1

Write the **consonants** in each of these words.

a) pencil   _____

b) computer   _____

c) crocodile   _____

d) holiday   _____

Activity 2

Write the **vowels** in each of these words.

a) house   _____

b) television   _____

c) nurse   _____

d) kangaroo   _____

Investigate!

Write your own words using **vowels** and **consonants** in the places shown. How
many words can you find for each pattern?

Here is an example.

c	v	c	c	v	v	c
b	e	d	r	o	o	m

a)

c	v	c

b)

c	v	v	c

c)

c	c	v	c

© 2016 Rising Stars UK Ltd.

2 Word classes

We need to know what the **word classes** are so that we can talk about how words are related and how they can be changed from one class to another.

- A **noun** is a naming word.

  table, banana

- An **adjective** is a describing word.

  huge, beautiful

- A **verb** is a doing or being word.

  jumped, was

- An **adverb** adds information to a verb, explaining how the action is done.

  quietly, kindly

Activity 1

Look carefully at the picture and then use it to give examples of the word classes below.

a) Write at least four **nouns** to show what you can see.

b) Think of a **noun** for something other than an object (a feeling).

c) Write at least four **adjectives** to describe what you can see.

d) Write at least four **verbs** to show what the people are doing.

e) Write at least four **adverbs** to go with the verbs you chose.

Investigate!

Look around the classroom and write down what you can see, using an **adjective** and a **noun** for each thing.

  tidy table, tall cupboard, quiet children

© 2016 Rising Stars UK Ltd.

3 Words ending in dge and ge

When you hear a *j* sound at the end of a word, it is spelled using either **dge** or **ge**. There are no English words that end in the letter **j**.

- **dge** is used after short vowel sounds (like the vowel sounds in **cat**, **tin** and **cup**).

- **ge** is used after consonants and also after long vowel sounds (like the vowel sounds in **shape**, **kite** and **cube**).

Activity 1

Do these words have the correct endings? Sort them into two columns, ✓ and ✗. Rewrite the words in the ✗ column to show the correct spelling.

	✓	✗
slege		
arrange		
edge		
randge		
huge		
cage		
chardge		
rige		

Activity 2

Choose the correct word or words to complete each sentence.

fridge   porridge   hinge   orange   fudge   challenge   strange

a) The piece of _____ tasted smooth and creamy.

b) Goldilocks ate all of Baby Bear's _____.

c) It was going to be a difficult race, a real _____ for her.

d) The _____ was broken, so the door wouldn't open.

e) The _____ juice tasted _____, even though it had come straight from the _____.

© 2016 Rising Stars UK Ltd.

4 Words with g before e, i and y

When you hear a *j* sound at the beginning or in the middle of a word, it is sometimes spelled with a **g**.

- The *j* sound is always spelled with a **j** before **a**, **o** and **u**.
- The *j* sound is often spelled with a **g** before **e**, **i** and **y**.

Activity 1

Is it a **j** or is it a **g**? Use the spelling tips to help you to decide. Change any incorrect spellings.

a) The fairy's wand had a <u>majic</u> <u>jemstone</u> in the middle.

b) <u>Imajine</u> a story of a <u>jentle</u> <u>jiant</u> living in a <u>jigantic</u> house.

c) The <u>jerbil</u> watched as the <u>jinjerbread</u> man <u>jogged</u> down the street.

d) The <u>jentleman</u> was looking forward to going on a safari to see some <u>jiraffes</u>.

e) If he caught any <u>jerms</u>, he may have to <u>adjust</u> his plans.

f) You need <u>enerjy</u> if you want to <u>goin</u> the <u>jym</u>.

g) It needed a <u>jenius</u> to mend the car <u>enjine</u>.

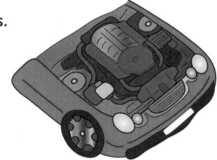

Activity 2

Which word can be used to complete both of these sentences?

The _____ led his army to victory.

As he read a lot of non-fiction books, his _____ knowledge was very good.

Investigate!

Find three more words that start with the *j* sound and begin with **j**, and three more words that start with the *j* sound but begin with **g**.

5 Words ending in le, el, al, il

When you hear an *l* sound at the end of a word, it is most often spelled **le**, but it can also be spelled **el**, **al** or **il**. There are very few rules to help you to learn these words, but here are two clues.

- The **el** spelling is used after **m**, **n**, **r**, **s**, **v**, **w** and usually after **s**, as in **tinsel**, **squirrel**.
- There are only a few words making this sound which end in **il**, such as **daffodil**, **council**, **nostril**.

Otherwise, these words just have to be learned by heart.

Activity 1

Decide on the correct ending for each of these words and write the full word in the correct box.

nostr   anim   cam   kett   met

app   tow   ank   chann

le	el	al	il

Activity 2

Choose the correct spelling to complete each sentence.

a) Rome is the _____ city of Italy. (capitel/capital)

b) A smooth _____ lay on the beach. (pebbil/pebble)

c) It was David's job to feed the family's pet _____. (gerbil/gerble)

d) The beautiful _____ was the queen's home. (castle/castil)

e) They found a _____ when they were digging in the quarry. (fossal/fossil)

© 2016 Rising Stars UK Ltd.

Activity 3

Choose the correct word to complete each sentence.

hospital   enjoyable   pupil   tunnel   medal

pencil   puzzle   bicycle   travel

a) Cara rode her _____ along the street.

b) The blunt _____ needed to be sharpened.

c) As the train went through the _____, everything went dark.

d) Everyone agreed that it was a very _____ meal.

e) Maryam had to go to _____ when she broke her arm.

There are four words left over. Write four sentences of your own using one of these words in each sentence.

_____

_____

_____

_____

Investigate!

Find words ending in **le, el, al** and **il** in story books. Write a list for each spelling. Which ending has the longest list? Which ending has the shortest list?

9

6 i and y words

There are a few words which make the *i* sound (as in **pin**) but are spelled with a **y**, such as **gym** and **mystery**. These are words that will just have to be learned.

Activity 1

Practise writing these words using 'Look, Say, Cover, Write, Check'.

symbol   **mystery**   **typical**   **syrup**   **pyramid**

Activity 2

Choose the correct word or words to complete each sentence.

gym   **pyramids**   **lyrics**   **Egypt**   **mystery**   **crystal**

a) No one could understand what had happened, it was a _____.

b) The _____ of the song were really joyful.

c) The children looked forward to going to the _____ for PE.

d) She wore a beautiful _____ necklace.

e) We are going on holiday to _____ to see the _____.

Investigate!

If you are not sure about the meanings of any of the words on this page, look them up in a dictionary.

© 2016 Rising Stars UK Ltd.

7 ou words

The letters **ou** can make different sounds.

- u ——→ **double, cousin**
- ow ——→ **sound, lounge**
- oo ——→ **wound, mousse**
- or ——→ **pour, course**

When reading a word with this spelling, you need to decide which sound makes sense. Sometimes you may need to try out the different possibilities.

Activity 1

Say these **ou** words to your partner. List the words that make a *u* sound.

trouble	court	country	pounce	through
rough	four	young	shout	touch

Choose three of these words and write a sentence for each.

1) _____

2) _____

3) _____

Investigate!

Collect words from your reading that have the spelling pattern **ou**. Copy the table into your book. Sort them into the different sounds that they make.

u (double, cousin)	**ow** (sound, lounge)	**oo** (wound, mousse)	**or** (pour, course)

© 2016 Rising Stars UK Ltd.

8 ei, eigh and ey words

ei, **eigh** and **ey** all make the same sound – *ai*, as in **pain, trail, play**.

Say these words out loud using the *ai* sound.

sleigh   **they**   **vein**   **eight**

Activity 1

Choose the correct spelling to complete each sentence.

a) My _____ lives next door. (neybour/neighbour)

b) An eagle is a bird of _____. (prey/preigh)

c) The bride wore a _____ over her face. (veil/veyl)

d) He stood on the scales to find out his _____. (weit/weight)

e) The dog had been trained to _____ his master. (obeigh/obey)

f) Queen Elizabeth II had a diamond jubilee to mark 60 years of her _____. (reign/reyn)

Activity 2

Write two words that rhyme with each of these words. It doesn't matter which spelling the words have, as long as they make the sound *ai*.

a) grey   _____   _____

b) eight   _____   _____

c) vein   _____   _____

© 2016 Rising Stars UK Ltd.

9 Prefixes: un, in, dis, mis, re

Most **prefixes** are added to the beginning of root words without any changes in spelling. Adding the **prefixes un**, **in**, **dis**, **mis** and **re** changes the meaning of the word.

- **un**, **in** and **dis** mean 'not'.
- **mis** means 'wrong' or 'false'.
- **re** means 'again' or 'back'.

Activity 1

Add the **prefixes** to the root words.

un + kind = unkind

a) **un** + happy = _____

b) **re** + fresh = _____

c) **dis** + agree = _____

d) **in** + complete = _____

e) **mis** + behave = _____

Activity 2

Which **prefix** can be added to all of the root words in each set? Write the new words.

| | un | in | dis | mis | re |

a) hear   place   fortune   _____

_____   _____   _____

b) please   approve   appear   _____

_____   _____   _____

c) do   decorate   fill   _____

_____   _____   _____

d) afraid   able   breakable   _____

_____   _____   _____

© 2016 Rising Stars UK Ltd.

Activity 3

Write the opposite of each of these words, either by adding or removing the **prefix**.

a) _____ dislike

d) _____ unpleasant

b) tidy _____

e) correct _____

c) count _____

Activity 4

Complete these sentences to show that the **prefix re** means that something has been done again. One has been done for you.

I had to rewrite my story because <u>I spilt water on it</u>.

a) Mona's sister had to replace her toy because _____.

b) We recycle paper because _____.

c) James wanted to replay the DVD because _____.

d) The bricklayer had to rebuild the wall because _____.

Investigate!

Collect words with the **prefixes un, in, dis, mis** and **re**, sorting them into columns. You could start with the words on these pages.

un	in	dis	mis	re

© 2016 Rising Stars UK Ltd.

10 Prefixes: super, auto, anti

Knowing the meanings of **prefixes** can help you to work out the meaning of the word.

- **super** means 'above'.
- **auto** means 'self' or 'own'.
- **anti** means 'against'.

Activity 1

Match the correct **prefix** to each word.

super		matic
auto		septic
anti		sonic

Activity 2

Which **super** word is being described in each sentence?

a) A large shop selling food and household goods is a _____.

b) A character who has a special strength is a _____.

Which **auto** word is being described in each sentence?

a) The signature of a famous person is an _____.

b) A book of someone's life, written by themselves, is an _____.

Which **anti** word is being described in each sentence?

a) Going in the opposite direction of the hands of a clock is _____.

b) Avoiding the company of other people is _____.

© 2016 Rising Stars UK Ltd.

11 Prefixes: sub and inter

Use the meaning of the **prefix** to help you to understand the word.

- **sub** means 'under'.
- **inter** means 'between' or 'among'.

Activity 1

Which **prefix** can be added to all of the root words in each set? Write the new words.

a) view   change   net   _____

_____   _____   _____

b) heading   divide   merge   _____

_____   _____   _____

Activity 2

international   subway   submarine   interactive   interfere   subtitle

Which **sub** word is being described in each sentence?

a) If you cross a road by going under it, you are using the _____.

b) If you are on a vehicle under the sea, it is most likely to be a
_____.

c) If you are reading a caption on a cinema screen to translate the words, you are reading a _____.

Which **inter** word is being described?

a) If you can communicate with a game, it is _____.

b) If you get involved in something that is none of your business, you
_____.

c) If your train is travelling between different countries, your journey is
_____.

© 2016 Rising Stars UK Ltd.

12 Prefixes: il, im, ir

Some **prefixes** change so that the new word they make is easier to say.

- Before a root word starting with **l**, **in** becomes **il**.
- Before a root word starting with **m** or **p**, **in** becomes **im**.
- Before a root word starting with **r**, **in** becomes **ir**.

All of them mean 'not' or 'the opposite of'.

Activity 1

Write each word with the correct **prefix** and listen to how that sounds.

a) We wouldn't say <u>inlegal</u>, we would say _____.

b) We wouldn't say <u>inregular</u>, we would say _____.

c) We wouldn't say <u>inmature</u>, we would say _____.

Activity 2

Use a dictionary to check the definitions of these words. Then put each one into the correct sentence.

      impatient   **irrelevant**   **irresponsible**   **illegible**

a) That piece of information is _____ to the topic.

b) Please do that again, as your handwriting is _____!

c) The woman became _____ as she waited in the queue.

d) The head teacher told the pupils that they had been _____ when they covered the wall in graffiti.

Investigate!

Find the opposites of these words.

logical   regular   probable   legal   modest

© 2016 Rising Stars UK Ltd.

13 Suffixes: ing and ed

We add the **suffixes ing** and **ed** to make verbs. The rules are given below.

- For most words, we just add **ing** or **ed**.

- When the root word ends in **e**, this is removed before adding **ing** or **ed**.

  hike ⟶ hiking/hiked

- When the root word ends in a consonant, the consonant letter is doubled before adding **ing** or **ed**.

  pat ⟶ patting/patted

- When the root word ends in **y**, change **y** to **i** before adding **ed**, but *not* **ing**.

  copy ⟶ copied / copying

Activity 1

Choose the correct spelling from each pair.

a) **like**   likeing   liking

b) **hurry**   hurried   hurryed

c) **ride**   riding   rideing

d) **enjoy**   enjoied   enjoyed

e) **slip**   slipping   sliping

Activity 2

Copy the table and use the rules to help you to add the **ing** and **ed suffixes** correctly to each word.

	ing	ed
drop		
float		
smile		
cry		
decide		

© 2016 Rising Stars UK Ltd.

Activity 3

Add the **ed** endings to the words in brackets ( ) and complete the sentences.
Remember the spelling rules!

a) We (walk) _____ to the park.

b) The baby (cry) _____ all night.

c) Dad (bake) _____ a cake for Sarah's birthday.

d) She (hum) _____ along to the song as she

(listen) _____ to the radio.

e) Everyone (clap) _____ when the performance had

(finish) _____.

Add the **ing** endings to the words in brackets ( ) and complete the sentences.
Remember the spelling rules!

a) We went (shop) _____ to buy new clothes.

b) They will be (fly) _____ to Spain tomorrow.

c) Fatima was (write) _____ a letter.

d) In the playground, the children were (hop) _____,

(skip) _____ and (jump) _____.

e) Ben was (drink) _____ water while he was

(run) _____ the race.

Investigate!

Collect verbs ending in **ing** and **ed**. These could be words of your own or that you find in books. Write them down and decide which rule was used to add the **suffix**.

© 2016 Rising Stars UK Ltd.

14 Suffixes: er and est

The **suffixes er** and **est** are added to adjectives to compare them. They are **comparative adjectives**.

| big | bigger | biggest |

The spelling of the adjective does not change if:

- it has a short vowel sound followed by two consonants
  strong, stronger, strongest
- it has a long vowel sound
  clean, cleaner, cleanest

The spelling of the adjective does change if:

- the adjective ends in **e** – remove the **e** before adding **er** or **est**
  whiter, whiter, whitest
- the adjective ends in **y** – change **y** to **i** and add **er** or **est**
  happy, happier, happiest
- the adjective ends in a vowel followed by a consonant – double the consonant before adding **er** or **est**
  mad, madder, maddest
- an adjective has three or more syllables – **er** and **est** are not used to show the comparative. Instead, we use **more** and **most**.
  beautiful, more beautiful, most beautiful

Activity 1

Copy the table and fill in the missing **comparative adjectives**, following the rules.

hot	hotter	hottest
light	lighter	
dirty		
	braver	
		luckiest
	flatter	
safe		

© 2016 Rising Stars UK Ltd.

Activity 2

Complete each sentence using the appropriate **comparative adjective**.
Remember the spelling rules!

a) Ahmed is fast, but Mark is _____ than him.

b) I am hungry, but Tom is _____ than me.

c) The bus was _____, but the lorry was wider.

d) Lyra is young, Daniel is _____ than her, but Ada is

_____.

e) Monday was _____, Tuesday was _____, but
Wednesday was wettest.

f) Lewis was _____, Fatima was thirstier than him, but Jack was

_____.

Activity 3

Use **more** and **most** to complete these sentences.

a) The bronze ring was expensive, the silver ring was _____, but
the gold ring was the _____.

b) Jo's book was interesting, Aidan's book was _____, but Amir's
book was _____.

c) The maths test was difficult, the English test was _____, but the
science test was _____.

Investigate!

Use what you can see around the classroom to write comparative sentences for
these sets of adjectives.

a) long   longer   longest

b) noisy   noisier   noisiest

© 2016 Rising Stars UK Ltd.

15 Suffixes: ment, ness, ful and less

All of these **suffixes** begin with a consonant, so they are added straight onto the root word. However, when the root word ends in **y** and has more than one syllable – then an **i** is added first.

- play ⟶ playful
- merry ⟶ merriment

Activity 1

If **ful** means 'full of' and **less** means 'without', what do these words mean?

Painful means 'full of pain'.
Painless means 'without pain'.

a) Beautiful means _____.

b) Hopeful means _____.

c) Careless means _____.

d) Sorrowful means _____.

e) Thoughtless means _____.

Activity 2

Change these adjectives into nouns by adding the **suffix ness**. List the new words.

fair   foolish   happy   wicked   tidy

_____   _____   _____   _____   _____

Choose two of the new words and write each in a sentence.

1) _____

2) _____

© 2016 Rising Stars UK Ltd.

Change these verbs into nouns by adding the **suffix ment**. List the new words.

move   pay   improve   agree   treat

Choose two of the new words and write each in a sentence.

1) _____

2) _____

Activity 3

Which **suffix** can be added to all of the root words in each set? Write the new words.

	ment	ness	ful	less
a) home	fear	end	speech
	_____	_____	_____	_____
b) manage	enjoy	replace	govern
	_____	_____	_____	_____
c) foolish	plain	kind	aware
	_____	_____	_____	_____
d) forget	wish	fear	resent
	_____	_____	_____	_____

Investigate!

Copy the table into your book. Collect words with the **suffixes ment, ness, ful, less**, sorting them into columns.

ment	ness	ful	less

23

© 2016 Rising Stars UK Ltd.

16 Suffix: ly

The **suffix ly** is added to an adjective to form an adverb. As **ly** starts with a consonant, it is added straight onto most root words.

neat ——→ neatly

quick ——→ quickly

The exceptions are given below.

- When the root word ends in **y** with a consonant letter before it. Then the **y** is changed to **i**, if the root word has more than one syllable.

angry ——→ angrily

- When the root word ends with **le**, the **le** is changed to **ly**.

terrible ——→ terribly

- When the root word ends with **ic**, **ally** is added instead of just **ly**.

heroic ——→ heroically

Activity 1

Use the rules to help you to add **ly** to each of these words.

a) kind → _____

b) steady → _____

c) simple → _____

d) comic → _____

Activity 2

Choose an adverb to complete each of these sentences to show how the verb is being done.

a) The man drove the car _____ along the narrow road.

b) Jenny stormed off _____ after the argument.

c) The little girl stroked the cat _____.

d) _____, the door slammed behind them.

e) The rain began to fall _____.

© 2016 Rising Stars UK Ltd.

Activity 3

Write three **ly** words that could describe each of these verbs. You can use some of these examples to start you off, or any of the other **ly** words from this unit.

cheekily   **quickly**   **cautiously**   **selfishly**   **dramatically**

played   **joyfully**   **fairly**   **nervously**

a) walked _____   _____   _____

b) ate _____   _____   _____

c) shouted _____   _____   _____

d) laughed _____   _____   _____

Activity 4

Write four sentences, using the verb and one adverb from each set above.

a) _____

b) _____

c) _____

d) _____

Investigate!

How do authors use adverbs ending in **ly** effectively? Find some examples in books, and write down both the adverb and the verb that it is describing.

© 2016 Rising Stars UK Ltd.

17 Suffix: ation

The **suffix ation** is added to verbs to form nouns.

- When the verb ends in a consonant, just add **ation**.

  expect (verb) becomes **expectation** (noun).

- When the verb ends in **e**, the **e** needs to be dropped before adding **ation**. This spelling pattern is more common.

  adore (verb) becomes **adoration** (noun).

- Exceptions: **publish** (verb) becomes **publication** (noun) and **cancel** (verb) becomes **cancellation** (noun).

Activity 1

Change each verb into a noun by using the **suffix ation.** Remember the spelling rules!

a) tax → _____

b) sense → _____

c) create → _____

d) prepare → _____

e) reserve → _____

Activity 2

Complete each sentence with the correct noun or verb. The words in **bold** will help you.

a) I had to **inform** her of my address, I gave her _____.

b) Let's **celebrate** Matthew's birthday, we'll have a _____.

c) I want to _____ the mountains, I'll go on an **exploration**.

d) Schools are here to **educate**, they give pupils an _____.

e) The doctor had to **operate**, he carried out an _____.

f) The football league will _____ the bottom team, there will be a **relegation**.

© 2016 Rising Stars UK Ltd.

18 Suffixes: multi-syllable words

When a word has more than one syllable, look at the last syllable to decide how to add a **suffix** beginning with a vowel (**ing**, **ed**, **er**).

- If the last syllable is stressed and ends with a vowel and consonant (such as **et**), you double the consonant.

  for**get** ⟶ for**getting**   be**gin** ⟶ be**ginning**

- If the last syllable is not stressed, the consonant letter is not doubled.

  garden ⟶ **gar**dener   **li**mit ⟶ **li**mited

Activity 1

What's the rule? Decide if these words need to have a consonant doubled or not before adding **ing**. (Say each one aloud and decide if you stress the final syllable or not.) Copy the table into your book and complete it.

	Final syllable stressed? Yes/No	Add ing
begin	Yes	beginning
permit		
enter		
order		

Activity 2

Choose the correct **suffix** and rule for adding it, to complete each sentence.

a) Dan decided that he (prefer) _____ carrots to broccoli.

b) Laura (visit) _____ her cousins last weekend.

c) She was a (begin) _____ at swimming, as this was her first lesson.

d) They heard her (admit) _____ to the teacher that it was her fault.

© 2016 Rising Stars UK Ltd.

19 Word families

Some groups of words share the same root word but have different **prefixes** and **suffixes**.

These 'word families' can help you spell them as they follow a pattern.

The root word is **solve.**

Solve and **dissolve** are both **verbs**.

Solution and **solver** are both **nouns**.

Insoluble is an **adjective.**

Activity 1

Write the **root word** for each word family.

a) helpful   helped   unhelpful   helpless   _____

b) action   reaction   actor   react   _____

c) display   playtime   replay   playing   _____

d) direction   redirect   director   directed   _____

e) agreement   disagree   agreeing   disagreement   _____

f) unrelated   relation   relationship   relating   _____

Activity 2

Write the **verb** for each word family.

a) joyful   enjoy   joyless   _____

b) paid   payment   repay   _____

c) education   educated   educator   _____

d) believe   belief   disbelief   _____

e) builder   built   rebuild   _____

© 2016 Rising Stars UK Ltd.

Activity 3

Change the **root word** into the correct form to complete each sentence.

a) Junior was full of (happy) _____ when he won a medal.

b) He was being (care) _____ but he still dropped the plate.

c) It was an important question, so the head teacher had to give it serious (consider) _____.

d) The (grace) _____ dancer moved across the stage.

e) It was as if he had (appear) _____ from nowhere!

f) The Year 6 play was a fabulous (produce) _____.

g) She was (recover) _____ from her illness.

Activity 4

Read all four sentences carefully and then decide which different words from the same family will fit.

a) When an ink cartridge runs out, you have to _____ it.

b) I thought I'd put my glasses on the table, but I have _____ them.

c) Sabiya _____ the jigsaw piece carefully.

d) A church is a _____ of worship.

Investigate!

Can you collect word families and see which family has the largest number of words? You could start with words that appear in this book and discuss which can be changed by adding a **prefix** or **suffix**. Use reading books, a dictionary and a thesaurus to help you to add to your collection.

© 2016 Rising Stars UK Ltd.

20 Determiners: a and an

A **determiner** goes with a noun to give the reader more information about it. Examples of **determiners** are **a, an, the, this, those, our, all, any**.

The choice of **a** or **an** depends on whether the word after them begins with a consonant or a vowel.

- If the word begins with a consonant, **a** is used (**a cat, a beautiful ring**).
- If the word begins with a vowel, **an** is used (**an egg, an incredible storm**).
- Exceptions are words that begin with a silent **h** (**an hour, an honest man**).

Activity 1

Do these words have the correct determiners? Sort these into two columns, ✓ and ✗. Rewrite the words to show the correct **determiner**. One is done for you.

	✓	✗
a autograph		an autograph
an interesting book		
a blue car		
an grape		
a slippery eel		
an open window		
an stripy umbrella		
an hungry horse		

Activity 2

Complete each sentence by choosing either **a** or **an**.

a) She picked up _____ piece of paper from the table.

b) We saw _____ eagle at the zoo.

c) _____ ice-cream will cool you down on a hot day.

d) I chose _____ sandwich from the menu.

e) We thought it was just _____ ordinary day.

f) He was _____ fast athlete.

© 2016 Rising Stars UK Ltd.

21 Plurals

The rules for making plurals are given below.

For most words add **s**.

car ⟶ cars

For words that end in **o** add **es**.

tomato ⟶ tomatoes

For words that end in **y** change **y** to **i** before adding **es**.

baby ⟶ babies

For words that end in **f** or **fe** change **f** to **ves**.

scarf ⟶ scarves

Some plurals are irregular.

man ⟶ men

foot ⟶ feet

Activity 1

Circle the words in each set that are **plural nouns**.

a) chairs   pizza   miss   dishes

b) knives   daisies   football   woman

c) glass   days   children   fox

d) monkeys   classes   reads   flies

© 2016 Rising Stars UK Ltd.

Give an example to show each rule for making **plurals**. One has been done for you.

For words ending in ch, the rule is to add es. My example is torch → torches.

a) For most words, just add **s**. My example is _____ → _____.

b) For words that end in **sh**, the rule is _____. My example is _____ → _____.

c) For words that end in **y**, the rule is _____. My example is _____ → _____.

d) For words that end in **f** or **fe**, the rule is _____. My example is _____ → _____.

Activity 3

Write the **plural** of the singular word in brackets so that each sentence makes sense.

a) Katy lost her (key) _____.

b) In autumn, (leaf) _____ fall from the trees.

c) The twin (baby) _____ cried all night.

d) The birds flew into the (bush) _____.

e) The (wolf) _____ howled.

f) Ow! The (cactus) _____ hurt me!

Investigate!

We know that some plurals are irregular (they don't follow the rules). Can you find the plurals of these words? Discuss them in a group first and then check in a dictionary.

tooth   **mouse**   **person**

deer   **woman**

© 2016 Rising Stars UK Ltd.

22 Apostrophes for contraction

A **contraction** is where two words are shortened to form a single word. The **apostrophe** shows where a letter or letters would be if the words were written in full.

didn't ⟶ **did not**

he's ⟶ **he is**

Activity 1

Write the missing words or **contractions**.

a) have not → _____

b) is not → _____

c) _____ → she's

d) _____ → couldn't

e) I have → _____

Activity 2

Rewrite each sentence, changing the full form to the **contraction**.

a) If <u>you are</u> waiting for Ellie, <u>she is</u> on her way.

b) <u>I will</u> meet you when <u>I have</u> finished my homework.

c) <u>There is</u> a new film at the cinema that I <u>cannot</u> wait to see.

d) <u>We would</u> come with you but <u>we are</u> feeling too tired.

e) As <u>it is</u> raining today, I <u>will not</u> be going out because I <u>do not</u> want to get wet.

Investigate!

Contractions are often used when writing dialogue. Listen in to people having conversations around you, and write down some of the contractions you hear.

33

© 2016 Rising Stars UK Ltd.

23 Apostrophes for possession

Apostrophes for possession are used to show that something belongs to a noun. When it refers to a singular noun, the apostrophe goes before the **s**.

The watch belongs to the girl, so it is *the girl's watch*.

The chair belongs to the teacher, so it is *the teacher's chair*.

Activity 1

Rewrite each of these, making sure that there is an **apostrophe** in the correct place to show **singular possession**.

a) the dogs bone   _____

b) the babys bottle   _____

c) the cats collar   _____

d) the builders ladder   _____

e) the schools playground _____

f) Peters apple   _____

© 2016 Rising Stars UK Ltd.

Activity 2

Complete these sentences to show belonging. Remember to include the **apostrophe**. One has been done for you.

My sister owns a car, so it is <u>my sister's car</u>.

a) The girl took a drink to school, so it was _____.

b) The child was given a computer, so it was _____.

c) The footballer wore his own boots, so they were _____.

d) Leighton has a birthday today, so it is _____.

e) The bird built a nest, so it was _____.

Activity 3

Rewrite each sentence, putting an **apostrophe** in the correct place to show belonging.

a) Jamila borrowed Jades book.

b) The goalkeepers save was amazing.

c) They went for a milkshake at Lolas Cafe.

d) Simons new car is blue.

e) The wind blew Monas hat off and it landed on the cats tail.

Investigate!

Play 'Who does that belong to?' with a partner. Take it in turns to ask the question, with the other person giving the answer. For example:

Question – 'Who does that book bag belong to?'

Answer – 'It's Matt's book bag.'

Then, you both write the answer down, putting the apostrophe in the correct place.

© 2016 Rising Stars UK Ltd.

24 Homophones and near-homophones

Homophones are words that sound the same but are spelled differently and have different meanings.

bare and **bear**
night and **knight**

Some words nearly sound the same but are spelled differently, so they are **near-homophones**.

quite and **quiet**

Activity 1

Choose the correct **homophone** to complete each sentence.

a) When she saw the red traffic light, the driver put her foot on the
_____. (break/brake)

b) He had to hold on tight to the horse's _____ so that it would
stay still. (rein/rain/reign)

c) The joke was so bad, everyone let out a huge _____.
(grown/groan)

d) Faris was happy to _____ his certificate. (except/accept)

e) Mum liked to go and sit in the garden to get some _____ and
quiet. (peace/piece)

Activity 2

Match up each **homophone** to its meaning.

medal	the system set up to send and deliver letters
meddle	a person who is a man or a boy
mail	a metal disc given in honour of a special event, person or achievement
male	to get involved in matters that concern someone else

© 2016 Rising Stars UK Ltd.

Activity 3

Write a sentence for each word in these **homophone** pairs. Use a dictionary to look up the definition of any words you are not sure of.

weather/whether

_____

_____

heel/heal

_____

_____

scene/seen

_____

_____

Investigate!

Do you know the **homophone** partners for these words? Discuss in a group.

blue   one   plain   maid

37

© 2016 Rising Stars UK Ltd.

25 Word lists

In Year 3 and Year 4 you are expected to learn to spell a list of words. Here are some ideas on how to memorise them.

- Follow spelling patterns:

  address, **different** and **pressure** all have double consonants.

- Recognise prefixes and suffixes:

  accident<u>ally</u>, **actu<u>ally</u>**; <u>**dis**</u>**appear**, <u>**dis**</u>**belief**

- Practise words you use regularly in other lessons:

  eighth and **quarter** (in mathematics)

- Break words down into syllables:

  experiment ⟶ **ex-per-i-ment**

- Use a mnemonic, which is when you make a phrase out of letters of a word:

  because ⟶ <u>**b**</u>**ig** <u>**e**</u>**lephants** <u>**c**</u>**an** <u>**a**</u>**lways** <u>**u**</u>**nderstand** <u>**s**</u>**mall** **elephants**

- Use 'Look, Say, Cover, Write, Check' to learn words off by heart.

Activity 1

Break these words into syllables. Say them aloud, with a clap to show each syllable. Copy the table into your book and complete it.

Word	Break it into claps	Number of syllables
different	diff—er—ent	3
often		
continue		
remember		
particular		

© 2016 Rising Stars UK Ltd.

Activity 2

Which word in each set is the odd one out? Why?

a) pressure   difficult   popular   suppose   _____

b) position   ordinary   question   occasion   _____

c) play   eight   reign   weight   _____

d) arrive   decide   surprise   lie   _____

Activity 3

Practise these words using 'Look, Say, Cover, Write, Check'. Copy the table into your book and complete it.

	Look Say Cover Write Check
early	
increase	
calendar	
popular	
straight	

Now choose from the words in the table to complete each sentence.

a) Tom asked for an _____ in his pocket money.

b) Salt and vinegar was the most _____ flavour of crisps.

c) She had to get up _____ to catch the train.

d) Always use a ruler to draw a _____ line.

e) Mia made a note of her birthday on the _____.

Investigate!

Can you make up a mnemonic for these words and share them with your friends?

answer   opposite   heart   forwards

© 2016 Rising Stars UK Ltd.

26 Using a dictionary

Dictionaries can be used to:

- check the spelling of a word
- check the definition (meaning) of a word.

They are set out in alphabetical order. You need to use the first two or three letters to help you find it.

Decide comes before **describe**. Both begin **de**, but the third letter of **decide** is **c** which comes before the third letter of **describe** (which is **s**).

Activity 1

Put each set of words in **alphabetical order**.

a) arrive   address   appear   answer

_____   _____   _____   _____

b) extreme   early   eight   earth

_____   _____   _____   _____

c) continue   complete   century   certain

_____   _____   _____   _____

d) pressure   potatoes   possible   probably

_____   _____   _____   _____

e) difficult   decide   different   disappear

_____   _____   _____   _____

Activity 2

Only one word on each line is spelled correctly. Use a dictionary to help you to find out which one.

a) iresponsible   irrasponsible   irresponsible   irresponsable

b) quarter   quater   qaurter   quartar

c) internnational   intternational   innternational   international

d) operashun   operation   operasion   operattion

© 2016 Rising Stars UK Ltd.

Activity 3

Have a go at writing your own definition for each of these words. Then use a dictionary to check.

a) **Peculiar** means _____.

b) **Extreme** means _____.

c) **Grammar** means _____.

d) **Illegal** means _____.

e) **Fossil** means _____.

f) **Nutrients** means _____.

Activity 4

Now that you have checked the meanings of the words above, choose three of them and put each into a sentence.

1) _____

_____

_____

2) _____

_____

_____

3) _____

_____

_____

Investigate!

What are you learning about in other areas of the curriculum at the moment?

Use a dictionary to look up some of the words you have been learning. You can check the spellings and definitions.

© 2016 Rising Stars UK Ltd.

You can use a **thesaurus** to look up words with the same meaning as those you already know. This can help you to choose words to make your writing more interesting.

Here are some words that mean the same as **big**:

enormous, large, huge, colossal, tall, roomy, spacious

You will need to choose the one that fits best in your sentence. If you are writing about a giant, you might choose <u>huge</u> or <u>colossal</u>, but if you are writing about a house, you might choose <u>roomy</u> or <u>spacious</u>.

Activity 1

Use a thesaurus to find a list of adjectives that mean **nice**. Decide which would be most appropriate to describe these pictures.

We had a _____ time at the theme park.

What a _____ meal!

The view from our hotel was _____.

Activity 2

This set of words might be found in a thesaurus – but one shouldn't be there. Which one?

sprint   race   rush   crawl   hurry

© 2016 Rising Stars UK Ltd.

28 Fiction: characters

When you are writing a narrative, you need to build up a picture of what your characters are like. You can do this by thinking carefully about the words that you choose to describe them.

Words belong to everyone, so use the ones *you* like best to make your own writing more interesting!

You can choose from ideas you get:

- from reading and listening
- from work that you do in class
- when using a dictionary and a thesaurus.

Activity 1

You can use **nouns** to be specific about your character.

- 'The man' could be a *doctor, father, villain, wizard, footballer*.
- 'The dog' could be a *Rottweiler, Poodle, Dalmation*.

Choose from these nouns or use your own ideas to complete each sentence.

> **athlete**   **teenager**   **teacher**   **pirate**   **puppy**   **soldier**
>
> **musician**   **prisoner**   **goblin**

a) The _____ got up that morning.

b) The _____ walked along the beach.

c) The _____ opened her mail.

d) As the clock struck 12, the _____ froze.

e) When the _____ got to the end of the road, he turned right.

f) While the storm raged, the _____ waited.

© 2016 Rising Stars UK Ltd.

You can use adjectives to describe:

- what a character looks like, sounds like and even smells like!
  He was a <u>tall</u>, <u>muscular</u> man with a <u>low</u>, <u>booming</u> voice.
- how a character feels.
  She felt <u>nervous</u> but <u>excited</u> as she walked into the room.

Activity 2

Choose from these adjectives or use your own ideas to complete each sentence.

angry   pale   bony   wrinkled   bright   angelic   stern

young   stylish   scaly   mysterious   ancient

a) The _____ girl had a _____ smile.

b) Suddenly, the _____, _____ man appeared at the door.

c) The _____, _____ voice could be heard across the room.

d) Josh, a _____ boy, felt _____ and _____ on his first day.

e) The _____, _____ dragon flew towards the _____, _____ boy.

f) As the bus stopped, a _____, _____ person got up from their seat.

Activity 3

You can use powerful verbs to show exactly what a character is doing. For example, **The giant <u>ate</u> his food.** Or, **The giant <u>devoured</u> his food.** We get a clearer picture of what the giant did in the second sentence.

Choose from these verbs or use your own ideas to complete each sentence.

crept   fluttered   hurried   shrieked   trembled   wandered

stared   clapped   bounced   stumbled   smiled

© 2016 Rising Stars UK Ltd.

a) The elderly man _____ along the corridor.

b) High on the roof, the goblin _____.

c) The ballet dancer _____ across the stage.

d) Her eyes full of fright, Zahra _____ away.

e) As the ship moved away from the shore, he _____.

f) Glen _____ at the birthday surprise.

> You can use adverbs to describe the verb. This adds information to explain how a character is doing something. For example, **Elon walked down the street**. How did Elon walk down the street? **Elon walked down the street <u>quickly</u>.** Or, **Elon walked down the street <u>slowly</u>.** Using different adverbs can change the meaning of a sentence.

Activity 4

Choose from these adverbs or use your own ideas to complete each sentence.

patiently   hopefully   worriedly   viciously   dangerously

angrily   cautiously   joyfully   selfishly

a) She drove _____ along the road.

b) The doctor listened _____.

c) The wolf snarled _____.

d) _____, Charlotte waited at the hospital.

e) _____, the alien landed his spacecraft.

f) After overhearing his parents' conversation, the teenager walked _____ to his room.

Investigate!

Now practise putting all of these ideas together to write a paragraph about a character. Choose nouns, adjectives, verbs and adverbs to suit your character. If you think of a better word, that's fine – just neatly cross out your first idea and replace it. You've just edited your own writing!

© 2016 Rising Stars UK Ltd.

Non-fiction: instructions

The purpose of instructions is to tell your readers how to do something. You need to use vocabulary that makes it clear what they need to do and exactly how to do it.

- **Imperative verbs** ('bossy' verbs) tell readers what to do.
  stick, jump, paint, sew

- Time conjunctions tell readers what order to do things in.
  firstly, after, finally

- **Adverbs** give readers more information about the verb, explaining *how* to do it.
  carefully, neatly, boldly, clearly

How to make muffin pizzas

Ingredients: muffin cut in half, tomato paste, cheese, onion, a few mushrooms, courgette

1. Toast the muffin halves.
2. Slice the onion, mushroom and courgette.
3. Heat the oil and cook the sliced vegetables.
4. Spread the tomato paste on each muffin half.
5. Divide the vegetable mixture and place on top of the muffin halves.
6. Sprinkle grated cheese over the mixture.
7. Grill for 4 minutes.

© 2016 Rising Stars UK Ltd.

Activity 1

There are nine **imperative verbs** in this recipe. Identify them and write them down.

_____   _____   _____

_____   _____   _____

_____   _____   _____

Activity 2

Look at these **imperative verbs**. Which ones might also be used in a recipe?

sit   pour   shut   whisk   throw   listen   chop   boil   paint

_____   _____   _____   _____

Choose three of the other imperative verbs and write a sentence for each, giving an instruction.

1) _____

2) _____

3) _____

Activity 3

Instead of using numbers, we can use **time conjunctions** to show order. Begin each instruction with a time conjunction choosing from the list. You can only use each time conjunction once.

Finally   After   Next   Then   First   Now   Following that

a) _____, toast the muffin halves.

b) _____, slice the onion, mushrooms and courgette.

c) _____, heat the oil and cook the sliced vegetables.

d) _____, spread the tomato paste on each muffin half.

e) _____, divide the vegetable mixture and place on top.

f) _____, sprinkle the grated cheese over the mixture.

g) _____, grill for 4 minutes.

© 2016 Rising Stars UK Ltd.

Choose an **adverb** to complete each sentence, or use an idea of your own. You can only use each adverb once.

evenly   carefully   lightly   delicately   thinly

neatly   gently   smoothly

a) Toast the muffin halves _____.

b) Slice the onions, mushrooms and courgette _____.

c) Heat the oil and cook the sliced vegetables _____.

d) Spread tomato paste on each muffin half _____.

e) Divide the vegetable mixture and place _____ on top of the muffin halves.

f) Sprinkle the grated cheese over the mixture _____.

g) Grill _____ for 4 minutes.

Investigate!

Have a look at some examples of instructions from books and magazines and decide if they can be improved. You could try acting them out or even actually making something, to see if they work.

© 2016 Rising Stars UK Ltd.